e-mail.this.book!

e-mail.this.book!

The Cartoon Bank

Alfred A. Knopf   New York   1997

THIS IS A BORZOI BOOK
PUBLISHED IN NEW YORK BY ALFRED A. KNOPF, INC.

Library of Congress Cataloging-in-Publication Data
e-mail.this.book! / the Cartoon Bank. — 1st ed.
p. cm.
ISBN 0-679-45085-8 (hardcover)
1. Computers—Caricatures and cartoons. 2. Electronic mail
systems—Caricatures and cartoons. 3. American wit and humor, Pictorial.
I. Cartoon Bank, Inc.
NC1426.E2 1996
741.5'973—dc20 96-36408
CIP

Manufactured in the United States of America
Published November 25, 1996
Second Printing, October 1997

A Message from the President

(of the Cartoon Bank)

My fellow Americans, I speak to you today not as a Republican or a Democrat or as an Independent (though I am all of those and more) but as an ordinary citizen of cyberspace. An information-communication revolution is taking place right before our eyes, under our noses, and behind our ears where we often forget to wash. Suffice it to say that the information superhighway is here and the information superduperhighway is on the drawing boards. Though the pace of change is certainly frightening, you'd better stop standing there staring like a deer caught in the headlights, or you're going to become virtual roadkill.

Yes, it's a brave new world, indeed, and, as I write this on my 300 megahertz toaster and my elderly mother surfs the Internet on her cardiac pacemaker, I wonder if it's a good new world—but there's no doubt it's a funny new world. In my capacity as President and Commander in Chief of The Cartoon Bank, I've sent my cartoon commandos on a search-and-satire mission to explore it. (Some of the cartoonists refused my direct order to go and had to be executed. I just want to say here, publicly, that no one regrets this more than I but that it was necessary to maintain discipline.)

However, the ones who weren't executed had lots of fun exploring a wired world where the wires are definitely crossed. They found a new playground for Murphy's Law. A place where the creative incompetence of humans combines with the mindless power of computers to insure that everything that can go wrong will go wrong, only much faster than ever before. For concerned citizens this state of affairs is, well, cause for concern. For cartoonists it's cause for cartoons.

So, come on, join in the fun (that's a direct order—you'd be unwise to refuse it): first, by enjoying these cartoons yourself, and then by sharing them with your friends, coworkers, and even sworn enemies, whether they're across the hall, across the country, or across the world. How? Well, you could let people look over your shoulder as you laugh hysterically at the cartoons in the book, but this will engender hilarity only in your immediate vicinity. To really do it right you've got to—you guessed it—**e-mail.this.book!** (To find out how to e-mail these cartoons as well as view and print them from the accompanying CD, see the instructions at the back of the book.)

Bob Mankoff
President (and Commander in Chief),
The Cartoon Bank

P.S. The material in this book and the software on the CD are, of course, copyright-protected. The cartoons are for your personal enjoyment. As such, you can enjoy them and send them to people to enjoy an unlimited number of times. But, you cannot sell, transfer, or use the cartoons for any commercial purpose without contacting the proper authorities. If you do, rest assured, the proper authorities and their jackbooted thugs will contact you.

e-mail.this.book!

"The e-mail isn't functioning—pass it on."

1

"How thoughtful. Mr. Kessler sent a dozen roses."

3

"Sure, I'd like a prince and a castle, but it will probably be like a genetic engineer or a software designer in some high-tech community."

"Sorry folks—it's not what you ordered, but everyone is getting fettucine until we fix the computer."

"Be patient, madam. At this very moment, state-of-the-art computers are working to eliminate or aggravate your problem."

update@info.hiway.net

"Thanks pal, let me put you on my mailing list."

"Great graphics, Dave, but the answer is still no."

"He's like a Bill Gates without a Microsoft."

FRED PETERSON

MAIN MENU

"My novel has some rough spots but I think
it's the software I'm using."

15

"Granted, I don't have much formal education or any computer skills, Ma'am, but I *can* shoot an apple off your head at forty paces."

"Dennis, I would like to talk to you for a minute—off-line."

"Do me a favor, chief. Next time you carve something
in stone, have it spell-checked first."

"One of those freak power surges, boss. The whole
damn system is down."

22

"Marge, this is davelow@meth.smu.com and
anncann@bur.com—I met them on the Internet."

"I think I'll head back to the house for a
little Net-sex and a nap."

"I've contacted your husband. He's at http://hottalk.com
and wants to know what I look like naked."

"Don't panic. It's only a prototype."

"The bunny did not get the job because the bunny
is cute. The bunny got the job because the
bunny knows WordPerfect."

"If you can prove it was computer error, the Church
will be happy to grant you an annulment."

"Correct me if I'm wrong, but didn't the Yanks
win the series in '72?"

"Hewes, it's come to my attention that you've been using our Internet access to troll for babes."

"I hate you! You don't understand me and you
don't understand my software!"

"This is our laptop model."

"Well, get someone over here pronto—I can't afford
to have thousands of dollars of useless equipment
out of commission."

"At this time we would like to pre-board those passengers
with laptops over fifteen pounds."

"It's the next step in the laptop revolution."

"Fine, Al, and how are you, your charming wife, Joni;
your two wonderful children, Charles and Lisa, ages thirteen
and fifteen; and your delightful German short-haired
pointer, Avondale?"

"A computer virus ate my homework."

"According to the message on the Internet, if you
fold it correctly, then hold it up to the light, it spells out
'GET A LIFE.'"

"You can't just punch in 'Let there be light' without writing
the code underlying the user interface functions."

"Hold on a second, my printer's going nuts."

"The computers are fine, the staff's down."

"He bringeth the system up, and
He causeth it to crash."

"They call it an on-line service, but can it
bring you a drink?"

POWER OFFICE ANXIETY

C.Barsotti

Robert's software gets the better of him.

"This computer has hairballs in it again."

"We're neither software nor hardware. We're your parents."

THE GUY WHO TOOK A WRONG TURN OFF THE ELECTRONIC SUPERHIGHWAY AND WOUND UP IN A MICROWAVE OVEN IN DAVENPORT, IOWA

"Say! Here's our Mac!"

"It's the new dress code at IBM."

"He'll call you back in about an hour. Right now
he's reformatting his mind."

"You've unpacked, now you need to download."

"Just among us we goofed. But officially it will
go down as computer error."

"There's nothing wrong with your personal finance software.
You just don't have any money."

"Well, enough of the coy sexual byplay, Bobby. I've got to dive back into the data stream."

"I haven't read it yet, but I've downloaded it
from the Internet."

"I'm thinking CD-ROM, but CD-ROM noir."

"Sorry, bub. You're not in the database."

"On the Internet, nobody knows you're a dog."

"My generation married captains of industry.
Now, to be comfortable, a girl's got to find
the right computer nerd."

"... modem ... modem ... modem ..."

"Everything that was in that filing cabinet is now on this little disk. Except of course for my bottle of scotch."

"Breakfast will be a little late. Our computer's down."

"Dear Diary: Repeat yesterday's entry.
Delete 'ham.' Enter 'pastrami.'"

MOSES OF MIDTOWN

"Here's a computer-enhanced picture of my kids."

"The much-ballyhooed era of TV interactivity
took a step closer to reality today."

"Believe me, the e-check is in the e-mail."

"You are entitled to one call, one fax,
or one e-mail."

P.C.VEY

90

"Garbage in, garbage out!"

"I always thought *this* was virtual reality."

BILL GATES' WEALTH
12940012738.56
Your family's contribution 128.19
The Bill Gates Wealth Clock

Agee

In an unbridled frenzy he altered his
log-on ID to new depths of depravity.

AMERICA OFF-LINE

Special Presidential
Medals of Acknowledgment To . . .

Allen C. Kempe and Aaron Giles, who permitted their shareware programs ShowGIF and JPEGView to be used on the CD. Please send all your money to these guys because we didn't send any.

Hank Duderstat, who wrote and tested the e-mail instructions many, many times and, for all I know, may be writing and testing them still.

Sumner Jaretzki, Chief Archivist at The Cartoon Bank and Archenemy of Error, who, among a thousand other things, wrote the instructions for viewing and printing the cartoons from the CD.

Joe Dator and Pat Krugman, also of The Cartoon Bank, who helped Sumner with the thousand other things.

The gang at Knopf. I'm so grateful to all of them that I'm thinking of changing my name to Bob Manknopf.

Cory Scott Whittier, Sarah Whittier Mankoff, and David Rupert Hewes, whose love and support make the awesome burden of the Presidency bearable.

Requirements for Use of the CD

Hardware: A computer (Macintosh or PC) with a CD-ROM drive

Software: 1) An e-mail program that permits sending and receiving graphic files

2) An on-line service provider that permits sending and receiving graphic files

Instructions for Macintosh

(Note: The number at the bottom of each page corresponds with
the number of the cartoon on the disk.)

Place the **e-mail.this.book!** CD-ROM into your CD-ROM drive. When the
e-mail.this.book! icon appears on the desktop, double-click on it so this window appears:

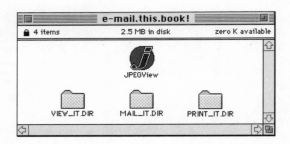

First, double-click JPEGView to launch it. You should see a dialog box
like the one below, except that the items listed will represent what's on *your*
computer. On the right you'll see the Desktop button. Click on it.

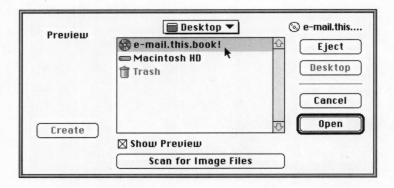

Next, double-click on **e-mail.this.book!** (If the Desktop button is dimmed, just double-click on **e-mail.this.book!**) Then, click once on VIEW_IT.DIR, then on Open (or just double-click on VIEW_IT.DIR). You will see two folders: B&W.DIR and COLOR.DIR.

Double-click on COLOR.DIR to open it. You will see:

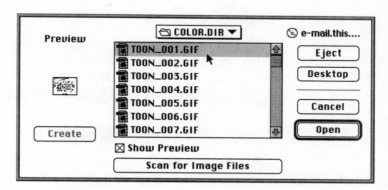

Then, double-click on any cartoon image file to view it. To see another cartoon, click on File (in the menu), then Open.

Printing is easy, too. Using JPEGView, open PRINT_IT.DIR, where you will find two directories: B&W.DIR and COLOR.DIR. In these directories, you will find the same cartoon images that were in VIEW_IT.DIR, except that these files are of higher quality (high resolution) and will look better when printed. Double-click on an image file in B&W.DIR to open it. Owing to its higher resolution, it will appear much larger on your screen than it will print. Click on File (in the menu), then on Print (below it). The cartoon you chose will be printed. (If you have a color printer, you can choose cartoons from COLOR.DIR also.)

Instructions for Windows

(Note: The number at the bottom of each page corresponds with
the number of the cartoon on the disk.)

Start Windows, and place the **e-mail.this.book!** CD-ROM into your CD-ROM drive.

Open the File Manager by double-clicking on its icon. (If you're unsure where File Manager is, read the manual that came with Windows.)

File Manager will allow you to access the CD in your CD drive. When you're looking at the contents of the CD, you will see the program SHOWGIF.EXE and three directories: MAIL_IT.DIR, PRINT_IT.DIR, and VIEW_IT.DIR. (In Windows, these names will appear uncapitalized.)

Double-click SHOWGIF.EXE:

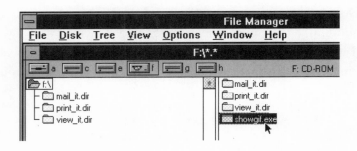

When the ShowGIF window opens, click on File (in the menu), and then click on Open:

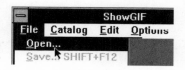

Next, double-click on VIEW_IT.DIR, and you will see two folders: B&W.DIR and COLOR.DIR. Double-click on COLOR.DIR. You will see all the color image files listed. The **.gif** extension on each file name indicates that they are all GIF (Graphics Interchange Format) image files. Double-click on any file to view it.

Printing is easy, too. Using ShowGIF, open PRINT_IT.DIR, in which you will find two directories: B&W.DIR and COLOR.DIR. In each of these, you will find the same cartoon images that were in VIEW_IT.DIR, except that these files are of higher quality (high resolution) and will look better when printed. Double-click on an image file in B&W.DIR to open it. Owing to its higher resolution, it will appear much larger on your screen than it will print. Click on File (in the menu), then on Print (below File). The cartoon you chose will be printed. (If you have a color printer, you can choose cartoons from COLOR.DIR also.)

E-mail Instructions

(Note: The number at the bottom of each page corresponds with
the number of the cartoon on the disk.)

E-mailing a picture to someone isn't quite as easy as cutting out the image in a graphics program and then pasting it into the text of the message you're sending. But it is relatively straightforward. The standard way that e-mail works is for handling text files. However, there *is* a way to send a copy of the cartoon using "attachments." Here are the steps involved to easy attachments:

The first thing you'll need to do is to find out some information about your friends, their computers, and what on-line service they use.

Here's what you need to know:

a) their e-mail address

b) their on-line service

c) the operating system of their computer (Mac or Windows)

Once you've collected this info and picked out the file you want to send, here's the process:

1) Open your on-line service's software or e-mail program and select the menu to create a new message.

2) Fill in the e-mail address of the person you want to send the file to (if it's not the same service as yours, you will need to use their *full* e-mail address, which is their user name combined with the "domain name" of their on-line service. It would read something like: bill@aol.com. (If an address includes an "at" symbol [@], you know it's a full address.) You'll also want to fill in the Subject and the Mail Message sections.

3) Then look for the button or menu to attach or send a file. Once you've found it, locate and select the file you wish to send (the cartoons are in the MAIL—IT folder on the CD). This is where their operating system is important. If it's the same as yours, no problem. If it's different—like you have a Macintosh and they have an IBM-PC— you should make sure to turn off any compression that your e-mail program would use.

4) Send the message . . . and with any luck it will arrive at your friend's computer with no problem. If there is a problem, that's where knowing the on-line service is important.

Not all on-line services handle attachments in exactly the same way. By the time you read this, 90 percent of the commercial on-line services should support the standard used by the Internet called MIME (Multipurpose Internet Mail Extension), and so sending an attached file from one service to another should be a snap. But there are some potential problems to be aware of. First, realize that MIME isn't the only game in town. Below is a list of the most popular formats for sending attachments (called "encoding").

MIME An encryption method that includes a description of what kind of file is being sent. Supported universally on the Internet and America Online.

Binhex A Macintosh standard identified by the suffix **.hqx.** If you're sending a file to a Mac and MIME doesn't work, use this format.

UUencode A UNIX standard that's especially popular for handling files (often called "binaries") in Usenet discussion groups. If you're sending a file to a PC and MIME doesn't work, use this format.

Base64 An older UNIX standard that's still very popular.

This is background information. Below is what's truly important. Remember, if you have problems sending a file within the same on-line service (say, both you and your friend are on America Online) the problem may be compression or just a bad transmission. Use this list to guide you in solving any problems that may arise between different on-line services. Use it to tell if your on-line service uses an encoding technique that is compatible with your friend's on-line service. If it isn't, then check to see if this can be changed in the Preferences menu, or use the manual method mentioned at the end of this article.

America Online MIME encoding (supported for only one file at a time). AOL will automatically compress multiple files, but be warned: if you are going to be sending files to a different operating system, make sure your friend has a copy of Stuffit Expander (Mac or Windows).

CompuServe Although MIME support is forthcoming, at this point you may have to manually encode the file on both ends of the transmission.

Prodigy MIME support is also on its way. Right now, files can be sent between Prodigy members only.

MSN Microsoft Exchange handles files in a UUencode format. The encoding and decoding process is automatic.

Internal E-mail Systems Most internal systems have no problem handling attached files. Only make sure that the setting matches the encoding type, and check out the systems capabilities before sending or receiving the file.

Internet MIME standard is fully supported on all e-mail programs. But if MIME doesn't work, use the Binhex format to send to Macs and the UUencode format to send to a PC.

The software used to manually encode and decode the attachments includes Stuffit Expander (Macintosh and Windows), UUencode and UUdecode (Macintosh), and Base64 (Macintosh). You should be able to find these programs in your on-line service's software area or on the World Wide Web at http://www.shareware.com.

Once the file is received on the other end, besides having the software to decode and decompress the files, the receiver may also want to actually look at them. Besides the usual commercial graphics applications, two other options include a web browser (any of them will handle GIF format; and Netscape, Internet Explorer, Enhanced Mosaic, Mosaic, and America On-line's Browser can all handle JPEG) or a shareware graphics program. Two of the most popular are JPEGView for the Macintosh and LView for Windows.

Index of Artists

A Note About The Cartoon Bank

The Cartoon Bank, Inc. is a computerized data bank of more than
25,000 cartoons from the most renowned cartoonists of our time.
It was founded in 1992 by Robert Mankoff, the brilliant humorist
whose work has appeared in *The New Yorker* since 1977.

If you have questions or comments about this book or The
Cartoon Bank:

Phone: 1-800-897-TOON
e-mail: bob@cartoonbank.com
Web site: http://www.cartoonbank.com

A Note on the Type

The text of this book was set in Electra and Bernhard Gothic.

Electra was designed by W. A. Dwiggins (1880–1956). This face cannot be classified as either modern or old style. It is not based on any historical model, nor does it echo any particular period or style. It avoids the extreme contrasts between thick and thin elements that mark most modern faces, and it attempts to give a feeling of fluidity, power, and speed.

Bernhard Gothic was designed by Lucian Bernhard for American Type Founders in 1929. Bernhard Gothic was ATF's response to the overwhelming popularity of the new European modern faces like Rudolf Koch's Kabel and Paul Renner's Futura. Bernhard Gothic is characterized by open characters, long ascenders, low cross strokes on the E, F, and H, and an open loop on the R.

Alfred A. Knopf, Inc. Limited 90-Day Warranty

Knopf guarantees for a period of ninety (90) days following the original retail purchase of this book and CD-ROM *e-mail.this.book!* that the program is free from substantial errors or defects that will materially interfere with the operation of the program as described in the instructions. This policy applies to the initial purchaser only.

This warranty gives you specific legal rights, and you may have additional rights which vary from state to state.

Disk Replacement Policy

If any disk supplied with this book fails within ninety (90) days of purchase for any reason other than accident, misuse or lack of hardware and/or software requirements, please return the defective disk together with a dated proof of purchase to Alfred A. Knopf, Inc., c/o Random House Inc. Distribution Center, 400 Hahn Road, Westminster, MD 21157, for a free replacement disk. This policy applies to the initial purchaser only.

Limitations on Warranty

Unauthorized Representations:

Knopf warrants only that the program will perform as described in the instructions. No other advertising, description or representation, whether made by a Knopf dealer, distributor, agent or employee, shall be binding upon Knopf or shall change the terms of this warranty.

Implied Warranties Limited:

Except as stated above, Knopf makes no other warranty, express or implied, regarding this product or the instructions. Knopf disclaims any warranty that the software is fit for a particular purpose, and any implied warranty of merchantability shall be limited to the ninety (90) day duration of this limited express warranty and is otherwise expressly and specifically disclaimed. Knopf does not warrant either that the product or instructions will satisfy the requirements of your computer system or that the product will not cause damage, interruption or interference with your software, data or hardware. Some states do not allow limitations on how long an implied warranty lasts, so the above warranty may not apply to you.

No Consequential Damages:

Knopf shall not be liable for special, incidental, consequential or other damages, even if Knopf is advised of or aware of the possibility of such damages. This means that Knopf shall not be responsible or liable for lost profits or revenues, or for damages incurred as a result of loss of time, data or use of the software, or from any other cause except the actual cost of the product. In no event shall Knopf's liability exceed the amount you paid for the book and CD-ROM. Some states do not allow the exclusion or limitation of incidental or consequential damages, so the above limitation or exclusion may not apply to you.

You are entitled to use the accompanying CD-ROM for your own use, but may not sell or transfer reproductions of the cartoons, the book, or the software to other parties, nor rent or lease them to others, without the prior written permission of Knopf. You may use one copy of the software on a single terminal connected to a single computer. You may not network the software or otherwise use it on more than one computer or computer terminal at the same time.